ON THE BATTLEFIELD

Poems By

Roderick D. Talley

www.rdtalleybooks.com

Las Vegas, Nevada

Cover Designed by Oluwatosin Adebayo

ISBN: 978-1-7342540-0-6 (print)
978-1-7342540-7-5 (ebook)

Copyright © 2020 by Roderick D. Talley

All rights reserved. No part of this publication may be reproduced, distributed, or transmitted in any form or by any means, including photocopying, recording, or other electronic or mechanical methods without the prior written permission of the publisher. For permission requests, solicit the publisher via the address below.

R.D. Talley Books Publishing, LLC
4882 W. Lone Mountain Rd.
Las Vegas, Nevada 89130
www.rdtalleybooks.com

Dedication

I'd like to thank God for guiding me, my wonderful bride, Ebony, for believing in my vision, my family & friends for supporting me and helping me to spread awareness of my brand, the numerous pastors, bishops and ministers in whom I've learned from, and the multitude of customers and supporters who've allowed me to be blessing to their lives.
I appreciate all of you.

Prayer

Lord, I want to take a moment to thank you for everything. Thank you for building my character through the trials, thank you for forgiving me of my countless mistakes, thank you for continually giving me grace, thank you for using me to share your love to others, and thank you for being patient with me and my progress.
    I pray that this book helps each and every person who reads it, no matter what their beliefs are. Please speak to their hearts. Give them peace of mind and comfort in whatever situation they are currently dealing with. Let them know that you are in control of everything. In Jesus' name we pray, Amen.

CONTENTS

Poetry as Art & Weapons (Intro) 7
How the Enemy Works 8
Time for Change 10
Passing Through 12
Rest In Chaos (R.I.C.) 13
Apologies for My Past Mistakes 15
Conquering My Goliaths 16
For the Victims 18
My Cities 20
Rough Starts 21
The Equation, Minus God 22
A True Test 24
Losing Battles 25
Allergic Reaction 26
Military Phase 28
Daring Faith 31
Carrying My Cross 33
Mind-Field 34
Resurrection 36
Eye of the Storm 37
Garden Weed Effect 39
Dirt on the Table 40
Revival 42
Earned, Not Given 43
Slippage 44
Memorial Day 45
My Daily Bread 47
Sense of Failure 48
Thank You, Lord 50
Conversation with Lucifer 51
Throwing Stones 54
Lines of Liberation 55
Rebuilding Mode (Outro) 56

POETRY AS ART & WEAPONS
(INTRO)

I recognize that the art of poetry is more than just
having the ability to mix words and lines that rhyme…
anyone can do this without providing any substance or meaning…
It's not about who has the loudest bass line
or who has the latest trending rhyme scheme…
The art of poetry involves the ability
to use poetry as a weapon,
and loading that weapon
with our thoughts and experiences as ammunition,
ammunition to fire our weapons with expressions
that'll not only help us to address
our thoughts, feelings, barriers and transgressions
but to also begin the healing process,
to review our mistakes and learn the lessons…
Doing this with care helps build our character
and enables other people to see the beauty in our struggles—
thus making our weapon return to a form of art…
better yet, *a masterpiece…*
masterpieces that'll have positive impacts on people
who read, hear, and view them for generations to come.

Hip-Hop and Blues were created
by intelligent people who realized this.
So, in this book we'll be revering back to these roots
to help describe our struggles as a human race,
our struggles with multiple internal and external battles.
God bless you all and enjoy.

How the Enemy Works

I was taught that the best way to defeat your enemy
is to learn and study the tendencies of your enemy…
I would like to address our common enemy
known as Satan, Lucifer, the fallen angel
who was cast down to the same planet
in which our feet are planted.

There was a time when Satan was God's most splendored angel *(Ezekiel 28:12-19)*
he was placed highly by God himself and was one of his most adored angels
But he allowed wickedness into his heart and his boasting pride led to his fall
he wanted to raise his throne above God's and obtain the highest seat overall *(Isaiah 14:12-16)*
His sinful actions led to him being cast down from his splendorous phase *(Luke 10:18-19)*
he and his servants were hurled down to earth
and have been working to lead the whole world astray *(Revelation 12:9)*
He is filled with fury and knows that his end is near *(Revelation 12:12)*
so he's working every day to keep us in a state of mental bondage and fear.

He comes only to steal, to kill, and to destroy *(John 10:10)*
constantly roaming the earth in search of people to devour
(1st Peter 5:8-9)

But the Lord informs us to resist the devil and he will flee from you *(James 4:7)*
allowing him to dwell in your life is the only way he becomes empowered.

He blinds the minds of unbelievers. *(2nd Corinthians 4:4)*
He tries to outwit us with schemes. *(2nd Corinthians 2:10-11)*
He masquerades as an angel of light. *(2nd Corinthians 11:13-15)*
He works to block your blessings. *(1st Thessalonians 2:18)*
And he sets traps to ensnare you. *(2nd Timothy 2:26)*

Now that you know how our common enemy performs
you can now face your battles better equipped
and when you feel like calling it quits,
remember that through Jesus, victory is already yours.

TIME FOR CHANGE

I'm sick and tired of seeing so-called adults who act-out in public,
disrespecting people for illegitimate reasons and feeling no remorse from it
yet when I confront them for their cursing and yelling some of the foulest words ever written,
they have the nerve to turn their nose up at me and claim their title as being a ***Christian***...

HOLD UP!!!!...

You mean to tell me that you claim to be a born-again believer in Christ,
yet you walk around like you're superior and refuse to treat other people right?!
Believing in Christ is only ONE of the steps you take while walking in your new shoes,
we must also follow God's teachings and the example that Jesus lived through
We do this by studying His teachings in the scriptures that the Bible portray,
then we put these teachings into action as we work to better ourselves each day
What we DON'T do is use this title as an excuse to continue in our old and crooked ways,
Don't you know that's how our "Divided States of America" was created in the first place?!?...

It's time to change your attitude,
It's time to change your perception,
It's time for you to stop getting offended
whenever someone confronts you with correction.
It's time for you to humble yourself
and begin taking more positive actions,
It's time that you become more thoughtful
instead of being quick in your demeaning reactions.
The term "Christian" means to be "Christ-like"
so we must work daily to walk firmly on God's path,
there's already too many people who've condemned themselves
by walking with one foot on and one foot off of His path.
I'm not saying that you won't make mistakes
and I know that this Christian journey is hard,
but do yourself and everyone around you a favor
by actually living up to the title of "Man or Woman of God."

Passing Through

Big bro called me today, informing me that our dad's biological father passed away
we weren't close, so I really didn't have much to think, feel or say
He dipped-out on my Pops when he was a small kid and re-appeared a few years ago
He was comedic and charismatic; we failed to establish a meaningful connection though
I lack respect for men who decide to run-out on their families
when a man does this, it hinders how beneficial they can be
My father learned his lessons of manhood from his stepdad and trial-by-fire
It's a shame how my grandfather didn't return until after my Pops was retired
However, men like my grandfather did give me a source of motivation,
They motivated me to work towards breaking this cursed circulation
of men passing through life, having babies and then deserting their families...
I decided at an early age that I would never disappear on my family
Although he was hardly around, I forgive him for his decisions
I never got to tell him that, but I hope he reflected on his decisions
and realized how many priceless moments he missed-out on in all our lives,
I also hope that he found God before he exited this life.

Rest In Chaos (R.I.C.)

I've been attending numerous funerals over the past few years
I've buried some former pleasures and issues, yet I didn't bury them with tears
In fact, I buried them with joy instead of mourning
their deaths
however, I later realized that they are still alive and remain to have breath,
they're just dormant and will remain alive as long as their master in Satan roams
throughout the earth,
so here I make my "condolences" to be known…

"Rest in chaos" to the pornography addiction that strangled my blessings for many years,
"Sweet nightmares" to the demon who kept me in a mental bondage that was caused by fear,
"Recline in fire" to the forces attempting to wreak havoc on my peaceful home,
"Unwind in turmoil" to the spirits constantly trying to upend me from my God-given throne…
"Rest in chaos" to the spirit of doubt,
"Rest in chaos" to the feeling of shame,
"Rest in chaos" to that punk Lucifer
who keeps trying to play with my emotions like it's a game…
"Rest in chaos" to the spirits behind the law enforcement officers who's killing our youth
"Rest in chaos" to the spirits behind the leaders who lie to the public and conceal the truth…

"Rest in chaos" to that anger issue my brother,
It no longer has control over you…
"Rest in chaos" to that depression my sister,
I speak joy and peace to come upon you…
I speak freedom from the chains of generational bondage that has hindered us,
And to the demons who think I'm going to waste anymore ink on them—
"REST IN CHAOS" in the mighty name of Jesus!!

APOLOGIES FOR MY PAST MISTAKES

I've had the privilege of becoming friends
with some of the greatest people God has created
In fact, without their support and encouragement
to come this far, I never would have made it

I'm ashamed to come out and say
that I've ruined some of those friendships
I've lost some irreplaceable ties
with some great friends and relatives

I've hurt some men and women
who grew very close to me
And I apologize to everyone
who were left feeling broken from me

To the men in whom I abandoned during troubling times,
To the women whose trust I betrayed, halting our progression,
To the relatives with whom I failed to honor my promises,
I am deeply sorry. Please forgive me for my transgressions.

If it means anything, I've been praying for each of you,
praying that God would help you get through
those daunting phases of life that I left you in,
and that He would fully heal those wounds that I left in you.

Conquering My Goliaths

I always knew there had to be a better life than what I saw
I was determined to not be hindered by anything at all…
All the people who claimed they could see a future rocking with me
yet their supportive words turned into acts of doubt and envy
Teachers who labeled me as a lost cause,
Positive leaders who responded with negative withdraws,
Lucifer convincing me that I'm less than royalty
even though the definition of my first name is
"famous royalty",
The addictions that were supposed to end my life,
the mistakes I made that I weren't supposed to make right,
the achievements I was told I would never achieve,
the faith I wasn't supposed to have in order to believe
that I was meant for a greater purpose than running the streets
and that I wasn't supposed to sit back and settle for defeat,
The distractions formulated by our common enemy
that were designed to keep me in a mental state of poverty-
while keeping me from writing my poetry
that would encourage and inspire each person who takes time to read
my words, and allowing God to use me to plants seeds
into their souls, and discourage me from using my gifts and changing the world…
but God apparently has a better purpose for me while I'm in this world.

How do I know?

Because He has constantly pulled me out of muddy situations when my feet lost their grip,
He has constantly diverted bullets aimed at me from close-range that shouldn't have missed,
He constantly revived my courage whenever I lost it and wanted to give-up and quit,
He has constantly declared me as 'Not Guilty', and keeps having my sins acquitted,
He has constantly cleaned-up my mess and given me clean slates with his grace,
He has constantly blessed me although I know I never deserved them in the first place,
He constantly helps me to overcome barriers, He has constantly healed my diseases,
He has constantly renewed my strength despite the various battles I face in different seasons,
He hasn't deserted nor forsaken me, just like his Word says,
He's provided all the tools I need to pick myself up and continue to press
I don't know what barriers you're facing or the forces currently opposing you
but I encourage you to stay positive because God has his hand covering you,
and if He's done all of this for me, then He'll definitely do more for you.

For the Victims...
(Prose)

To the victims of sexual assault...
To the victims of domestic abuse...
I'm with you, standing by your side...
Feel free to call me when you need comfort,
Feel free to look up to me for guidance,
Feel free to view me as one of your protectors,
Feel free to cry on my shoulders,
Feel free to ventilate your anger, your pain,
your confusion, sadness and humiliation around me...
I'm not half the man Jesus is but I put your sorrows
on my back
as well as the sins of the abusers...
I know some of you sought comfort from others
in your times of vulnerability
yet they used that against you for their
personal satisfaction...
Some of us people
may not know the potential of our strength
but we know we're able to cause
serious damage
and don't need to put our hands on other people
just to prove it...
To the victims of sexual assault,
To the victims of physical, verbal and emotional abuse,
I pray that you have found it in your heart
to forgive your oppressors
so that the bitterness doesn't engulf your spirits...

Forgiving others doesn't mean you have to
forget what they've done and trust them again…
but turning over all your hurt, anger, and bitterness to God
will enable the healing process to begin…
That situation that should've "taken you out"
will become your testimony if you allow it…
A testimony that will help other victims
follow in your footsteps.

God bless you, my friends.
My prayers are with you all.

My Cities

Tulsa, Cincinnati, Middletown and Dayton,
before adulthood, these were the cities I grew-up in
Knew at an early age that my childhood wouldn't be all roses
bore witness to numerous atrocities, including betrayal
by our closest
Witnessed the effects of prostitution, drug addiction
and violence,
church-people who acted disorderly, but everyone kept their
sins in silence
Lived through the detrimental effects of an ugly divorce
the negativity took root in me as I joined the madness
with no remorse
When I later learned the tumultuous histories behind
each of these cities
I realized that I came up during the "post-war era"
of these cities
My family and I have experienced some trauma while living
in these places
yet somehow, despite it all, we've been able to keep smiles
on our faces
I don't regret my upbringing because I've learned
so much from it
with the joy I've obtained, I want to help these cities
experience some of it
I'm anxious to help each of these cities become
more productive
I just don't know where to start as of yet but stay tuned,
because with God's help, there's no telling what kind of
plans we'll come up with.

ROUGH STARTS

I'm just not feeling it today…
Been feeling out of sync since the moment I woke up,
I'm already distracted by multiple things and the sun
ain't even fully up
Already running late for a couple of appointments,
today I'm just feeling like I'm a big disappointment…
Don't feel like being a positive person,
I just feel like swinging my fists and cursin'
Been reading a couple of guidance books and devotionals,
frustrated that it feels like the lessons haven't taken root at all
I feel like I'm distant from my heavenly father,
I don't feel his presence and it's got me quite bothered
Today I don't feel like being a soldier in the
Army of the Lord,
today I don't feel like wielding my indestructible sword
Pray for me, because I don't feel like fighting and being a good soldier,
but the love of God is what has kept my heart from becoming heavy like a boulder…
I know very well that I am far too blessed
to allow this feeling to dwell throughout the day
and indulge in its mess.
I can hear the Lord saying,
"Wake-up King!!, this is only a test."
"Wake-up Queen!!, this is only a test."
"Rise-up out of that place of shame, doubt and duress!!"
"Get back to fighting the Good Fight and continue to press—
and get ready for the new thing I'm about to do in your life next!!"

The Equation, Minus God

To the entrepreneurs and business reps who are pressed
because the desired results are not reflecting your efforts
yet...
You've been trying to conduct business in the correct way
yet the people who are bending and breaking the rules
seem to be reaping more profitable days and better pay...

To the artists who are speaking and displaying God's truth
through their art,
yet you keep getting overlooked by other people
who praise other artists for wanting to remain in the dark...
You want to use your light to expose this dark industry
and call-out these hyped-up artists for the fake artists they
really are...
You want to tell them face-to-face that they have no heart
and punish them for disrespecting the meaningful culture of
real art...

I know it's tempting to take God out of the equation and take
matters into your own hands,
I know it's tempting to push God to the side and deviate
from His plan
but if we take God out of the equation then we'll lose sight
of our purpose,
we'll fall into Satan's trap and all of our hard work will
become worthless
Understand that a lot of people just want to ignore God and
do things their own way,
know that Satan roams the earth looking to blind people
from the truth and lead them astray

Therefore, we must continue being beacons of hope and rise above our flesh
and remember that the Lord is returning soon to put Satan's nonsense to rest.

A True Test

Learning how to wait on God
even when we don't feel his presence,
Allowing this skill to be developed in your life
brings its own level of relief and essence

I was once told by a great Man of God
that this was the highest order of discipline,
I realized that, even to this day, that
this is a common struggle amongst us humans

Our society applies pressure for quick results
creating minimal room for growth and patience,
often missing the lessons and beauty of our situations
and places,
while, in return, making us more stressed, tired, and anxious

One characteristic about God is that
his timeline doesn't conform to this world's timeline,
Although our world tends to rush things,
he still moves on *His* time, yet He's always on-time

There's an indescribable feeling of reward and comfort
when you develop yourself to trust and wait on God,
I encourage you to build your patience, and to focus
on the various tests and lessons that are implemented by
God.

Losing Battles

Losing our loved ones…
Losing our close, loved ones truly hurts,
especially when they never got the full view of their
Godly-worth,
especially when it's someone you've known since their birth,
or worse, someone in whom you created and gave birth…

I've dealt with death several times
so you'd figure I would be used to it by now,
and although I take pride in being a rock in my family
it's becoming more and more difficult to deal with
somehow…
Not to mention that we can't seem to ever find the
words to say
that'll make the grieving people feel ok…

Our emotions are the deepest when someone we know
passes away
probably because we humans were considered
God's most precious and valuable
creation from the very first earthly day…

Always pray for the families who have lost loved ones.
Pray that God grants them comfort, peace of mind,
and strength to get them through their tumultuous times.

Allergic Reaction

I can't do it...
I can't be around people who don't have a positive mindset
like me,
I can't be around people who act fake when they're not in
front of me
I used to be able to tolerate their nonsense,
I used to allow myself to be drawn into their nonsense
I used to let myself be hindered by their negativity,
I used to partake with them in spreading negativity
But now, hanging around them too long makes me sick
to my stomach—
almost to the point I want to vomit,
Sometimes I can smell the stink of their presence
from a distance,
and sometimes it smells just like vomit...
I'm not referring to people who are working towards a better
life and productive change,
I speak of the people who choose to remain stuck in their
demeaning ways and refuse to change
Whenever the people in my company try to start
spreading gossip,
my spirit reacts and I can't help but to make them
cease the gossip
Whenever people in my company try to bring up my past
mistakes to make me feel guilty,
I admit those mistakes and remind them that God forgave me
and declared I'm not guilty,
Whenever people in my company tries to talk-down on
someone and discredit their image,

I interrupt their party and educate them on how we were all created in God's image
Whenever Satan tries to use someone in my company to attack my character and personality,
I gently but firmly remind them that it was God himself who gave me this personality
So if you think you can bring any type of pain, curses, drama or foolishness upon me,
just know that I'd rather love on you…but I'm warning you, please don't try me.

Military Phase

Eighteen years old, feeling patriotic, ready to see the world and full of optimism,
excited to taste some freedom like a man who was getting released from prison
Signed up for the Marines the year prior at the age of seventeen,
wasn't fond of going to college but I was still anxious for a new scene
Seemed like some of the people back in Ohio tried to keep me boxed-in,
my outgoing personality couldn't be tamed as I sought some new friends,
Received my first check after boot camp and thought my struggles were at an end,
connected with other young men from different states, learning of their troubling trends,
met several ladies who found me attractive, ready to enjoy life and party,
most of us were celebrating the fact that we had finally escaped poverty…

Although I had successfully escaped the peculiar troubles of childhood,
I soon realized that I had entered into the common troubles of manhood,
Adversity stuck with me as I encountered opposition from men twice my age,
some of my superiors tried vigorously to hinder my advancement—
causing me to realize that maturity doesn't come with age,

The same fact was discovered with some of the older women
I became fond of,
some of them quickly claimed to be pregnant when I didn't
use a "protective glove"
some of them played numerous mind games,
some pulled disappearing acts like smoke in mirrors,
some I later discovered were disgruntled wives, still involved
in broken marriages,
I even dealt with the horrifying phase of one of my
girlfriends having a miscarriage…

The sour and untrustworthy taste that formed in my mouth
over time
caused me to speak ill words to close-ones and destroy
relationships with true friends of mine…
of course, I realized my stupidity and the consequences it
had after the passing of some time…
I realized the detrimental effects that came with continuous
time away from your family,
it troubled me to see the amount of people that divorced their
spouses and families,
It was funny how I spent more time trying to defend myself
and my dignity
when I was actually getting paid to defend the freedom
of my country…

Despite the constant ups and downs, the madness I witnessed
and experienced,
I realized that God had me covered throughout the
whole experience,

Despite the friendships that were derailed from the numerous unforgiveable situations,
some of my best friendships today were established in the midst of those unfortunate situations,
My eyes were opened to the fact that this world doesn't agree with my character,
I realize that God used those four years to jump-start the process of building my character.

DARING FAITH
(PROSE; INSPIRED BY PASTOR PAUL MONTANO'S SERMON "DARING FAITH")

Faith and fear cannot coexist…
they shouldn't even be in the same sentence…
The meaning and effects of these two words
are so opposite of each other
that they defy all of the laws
of math, science, gravity, legalities…and common sense…
You see, faith is based on truth and facts
while fear is based on assumptions of what may happen…
Looking at problems through faith
enables us to see and realize our victorious ending,
while looking at issues through fear
makes us exaggerate our problems
and not see them for what they really are…
Faith elevates our mindsets,
granting us peace of mind and comfort
and the ability to press forward and progress
through our trials…
Fear, on the other hand, puts us in a mental state of turmoil
and instability,
shutting down any kind of progress we may make…
Faith opens the doors for God's miracles
while fear opens the doors for Satan's attacks…
Faith moves God to act on our behalves,
faith unlocks the promises of God,
faith turns God-given dreams into reality…
Faith is NOT a desire,
It is NOT you pretending to believe in a lie,
It is NOT a feeling,

It is NOT you bargaining with God,
It is NOT you saying, "I'll believe it when I see it"…
Faith is NOT society's definition,
which intends to keep you in a "boxed-in" state of mind…
In fact, faith dares you to trust God and operate
"outside the box"
and I dare you all to step-out of your comfort zones
and tap into this level of faith.

Carrying My Cross

Thank you, Jesus, for saving us by enduring the pain and dying on that cross
and please give me strength as I take-up and carry my cross…
Don't allow my flat-soled feet to stumble as they become sore and weary,
strengthen my back and legs as I take on other people's burdens—
and my cross becomes more and more heavy…
Allow my brothers to apply their burdens to my cross, even as I make my way up this rocky hill,
allow my sisters to apply their sorrows as I'm weighed down by the weight of their tears,
allow my friends to pass their illness to me as it weakens my immune system,
allow my enemies to place their hatred on me, adding the weight of the world's corrupt system…
If this leads to my brothers experiencing freedom from bondage, then so be it
if this allows my sisters to experience joy and happiness, then so be it
if this leads to my friends living stronger and healthier lives, then so be it
if this leads to my enemies becoming people who love on each other, then so be it…
You've already blessed me abundantly Lord, now I wish to share your love to a dying world,
I wish for others to experience your unconditional love and indescribable presence—which extends far beyond the understanding of this dying world.

Mind-Field

(Inspired by Min. Andrew Cox's sermon, "Ready for War")

We all could sense it, both Christians and non-believers
that there is a constant warfare happening in our lives,
having us in constant need of stress and pain relievers…

It started back when Satan influenced Adam and Eve
to disobey God's command, causing our human race
to be deceived
Satan knew he couldn't defeat God, but he could influence
our decisions
he knew he could deter us from our journeys and distort our
focus and precision…
If you read the story in Genesis, this is how Adam and Eve
lost sight of God's vision.

It is important to realize that the primary battles we face are
within our minds.

Our mind is like a minefield,
and although our goal and focus can be clear,
our journeys will require us to side-step numerous mines
that Satan plants in the field.
Those "mines" are the millions of negative thoughts
that Satan will plant to influence your train of thought,
And if we don't continue to seek God's wisdom
then Satan will cause us to lose sight of our vision,
with distractions that'll take our attention,
knocking us off-course from our missions,
keeping us from fulfilling God's commission,

causing us to doubt our worth and our existence…
I pray that you arm yourselves daily with God's teachings, my friends
so you can stay focused and continue to press-on until this warfare ends.

RESURRECTION

In the year 2019, I had the pleasure of having my birthday
on the same day as Jesus' Resurrection/Easter Sunday…
I imagined Him sitting next to me on the couch when we
got home from church
overjoyed that the King of Kings was celebrating His
resurrection on the day of my birth…
I poured each of us a glass of one of my favorite drinks and
we made a toast
I congratulated Him on defeating death's grave and thanked
Him for giving us hope
He tilted His glass and then congratulated me on not
giving-up on life
He also thanked me for allowing Him to take residence and
guide my life
I told Him that I've made so many mistakes,
He replied "Yes, but your heart is in the right place",
I told Him that I'm not even half the man you are,
He said, "Just continue pressing towards my Father's mark"
I switched my focus and celebrated the fact that He
was in our presence
we also celebrated the fact that we both arose out of a
place of hindrance
I encourage you, my fellow readers, to use Jesus' example to
give you hope
in facing your tough situations and barriers so that you'll
overcome them and cope

Eye of the Storm

Evil, sadness, hatred, sickness, temptations…
all of this surrounds you on a regular basis
People curse you when you try to love on them,
people throw dirt on your name although you honor them
Relatives have distanced themselves from you,
close friends have turned their backs on you,
Constant threats give reason for you to quit and
sound the alarm,
however, despite the mess surrounding you,
you remain calm…
Seems like God is only one who cares enough—
enough to give you peace of mind and comfort,
the carnally-minded can't understand this new echelon
and question how you remain cool, calm and collected—
failing to realize that you got here simply by prayer.
God has placed you in the eye of the storm,
and through this eye, you are able to see
the situations for what they really are—
attempts to distract and diverge you from what you're
destined to be.
Times usually become more difficult before they get better,
you now realize that you're close to your next blessing.
My brother, my sister…
if this is you then keep your head up.
God has you exactly where he wants you to be
so keep pressing forward and please don't give-up.

"Dear friends, do not be surprised at the fiery ordeal that has come on you to test you, as though something strange were happening to you. But rejoice inasmuch as you participate in the sufferings of Christ, so that you may be overjoyed when his glory is revealed." -1st Peter 4:12-13, NIV

"If the world hates you, keep in mind that it hated me first. If you belonged to the world, it would love you as its own. As it is, you do not belong to the world, but I have chosen you out of the world. That is why the world hates you." -John 15:18-19, NIV

GARDEN-WEED EFFECT

I remember back in college while attending a session on growing healthy food
a few of us were helping a farmer harvest his crops and pulling weeds from around the food,
The farmer went into explaining the importance of removing all of the weeds
and why we needed to completely uproot them, not just cut the top part that we can see
He explained the nature of weeds, and how they take the moisture away from crops,
It's funny how I immediately realized how our lives as humans are similar to the lives of crops…
When we allow toxic people in our circle, they tend to drain the life out of us,
their demeaning character tends to infect us and our words become infectious
We become like bacteria, find reasons to mistreat other people and make a fuss
because we allowed our circle to become polluted by envy, hatred, dissatisfaction, and lust
My friends, please don't allow the ways of this world to drain your joyful moisture,
pay attention to the type of people you allow to influence your life and into your circle
If you're already in this situation, be quick to detach from them and dispose their negative roots
because if you let them stay, you too will soon be unable to produce righteous fruits.

DIRT ON THE TABLE

The unfruitful urges still arise suddenly yet they're occurring less frequently
my anger still flares-up at times yet my reactions are not as quick as they used to be
I'm not proud to admit that I've had a relapse back into pornography,
but I'm too determined to let these issues overtake my life and get the best of me
So please pray for me...

My sincere appreciation for women has proven to be my gift and my curse
as I sometimes find myself staring too long at other women's silhouettes and curves
I have the perfect wife, yet my eyes still sometimes struggle to turn away,
So I beg you, for my sake, please pray...

Lord, I need your help to fix this,
because I need to break this generational chain
and teach my future sons how to not live like this,
plus I know that I'm not the only man struggling with this...

Moments like this make me realize that I need to draw closer to you...
You've brought me a mighty long way
but there's still some areas in my life that I need to improve...

How do I do that?

I need to pray more, speak to you more,
trust in you more, learn from you more,
I need to spend more time reading and pondering
your scriptures,
I need to fellowship more with other like-minded Christians,
I need to continue seeking your guidance
and make more effort in seeing you in every situation,
also remind myself that I'm here today by your love, grace
and patience.

REVIVAL

Revive me, Lord…
This life-long battle on a planet that's heavily influenced
by our common enemy
has taken quite a toll on me…
Although there's people who have faced bigger challenges
than the ones facing me,
this fight has definitely drained my energy…
I remember reading in your Word how you'll place us in the
midst of our enemies
like a sheep amongst a pack of wolves,
yet it's discouraging seeing the amount of people who work
against me,
even though they share many similarities as me…

Revive my strength, Lord…
Revive my life, Lord…
Restore my joy, Lord…
Do the same for my wife, Lord…
An indescribable feeling of happiness came over me
when I first accepted you into my life—
Revive that happiness, Lord…
Revive my courage, Lord, so that my passion for you
will overflow and spill over into my work,
As I work to improve myself and encourage everyone
around me,
especially while I'm in contact with people
outside of church…
I thank you in advance, Lord.

EARNED, NOT GIVEN

You really want the title 'Man of God'?
You really want the title 'Virtuous Woman'?
These are the most honorable titles a man or woman
can ever earn,
but make no mistake, these titles must truly be earned
There's a lot of work that must take place in your life,
you're going to be tested and tried every single day and night
You're going to face opposition from people and directions
from all sides,
this is the reason why many Christians who begin this
journey soon backslide
You're going to be inflicted with pain that'll sometimes
feel unbearable,
people are going to betray you and treat you like you're
something terrible
You're going to be judged negatively by others and
you'll be an outsider
but as you study the Bible, you'll notice that Jesus was also
considered an outsider
You'll notice Jesus had people constantly watching him,
ready to scrutinize his every action
you'll notice people hated Him because they couldn't
understand his superior wisdom
God is going to elevate you as you persevere through the
numerous storms
some people will disconnect from you as you allow God to
mold your spiritual form
Keep trusting Him though and keep pressing towards his
mark, you'll soon reap the eternal rewards of this journey on
which you've embarked.

SLIPPAGE

So you nearly blew it, huh?
You've slipped-up and almost fell
for that trapping temptation, huh?
Pick yourself back up and dust that dirt off you, King
In fact, grab my hand and let me help you up, King
Many of us married men have faced the urge of chasing
another woman…
hell, even I almost fell for that same thing.
Even I have slipped-up and found myself
in the same position you're currently in.
If it weren't for God intervening,
who knows the size of the hole I would've dug myself in.
This is why we must continue to seek God's help daily
because our flesh alone is too weak to withstand
all of these tempting desires
that are attacking each and every married man.
Incorporate prayer more into your daily routine
because I guarantee you this test will approach you again.
It'll probably come onto you stronger next time,
So please be on guard, my friend.

MEMORIAL DAY

To those of us who have served in the armed forces,
Memorial Day is such a meaningful day…
many brothers and sisters in arms that we got to
know personally
were snatched from existence on many horrific days…
But as I think about those who have passed away,
those unfortunate people who have met their unruly fate
I can't help but recognize not only our fallen military people,
but those who were killed and beaten on some of our
country's "forgotten" dates,
Such as the tens of millions Native Americans and Africans
who suffered from the Europeans "discovery" of America in
the 15th century,
the Mexicans who also rapidly started losing their territories
to European expansion during the 16th & 17th centuries,
The victims of the New York City Racial Massacre in 1863,
The Atlanta Racial Massacre in 1906,
The East St. Louis Racial Massacre in 1917,
The Chicago, Knoxville, & Washington D.C. Racial
Massacres all in the year of 1919…
The Rosewood Racial Massacre that occurred in 1923,
Tulsa's Racial Massacre in 1921 that destroyed
Black Wall Street—
which happened to occur on the same weekend Memorial
Day is usually observed…
The National Guard even participated in some
of these incidents
but instead of working to increase the peace,
they took sides and fought against the Blacks

primarily because they felt that the Blacks
weren't deserving of a slice of wealth, or a rich
country's piece…
The military personnel who died in wars that had
invalid purposes,
the victims of the "war on drugs", which was really an attack
on the poor and defenseless
The victims of Standing Rock and other countless incidents
of police brutality,
the victims who've been struck down and harassed just
because they weren't the favored ethnicity…
The people who were blamed for crimes they didn't commit
and quickly became a statistic of the wrongfully convicted,
The many innocent men, women and children
who were simply at the wrong place when they
caught stray bullets…
My fellow Americans, I ask that you don't forget about these
unfortunate victims,
Please help me keep their memories alive
and not let the memories become forgotten
and buried with them.

My Daily Bread

There is no question about it God… you are my daily bread…
You don't need me to help carry-out your purpose and will
I'm powerless without you, yet you wanted me still…
I had nothing to offer you, but you wanted me still,
I had nothing to lose yet you blessed me still,
I saw no value to my life, yet you valued me still,
you even blessed me with a wife who views me
as perfect, still,
my actions don't deserve these blessings,
yet you shed grace still,
I've even cursed at you a few times, yet you love on me still…

Your unconditional love has changed me for the better,
I now walk, talk, think, perceive, and act better…
It's all because of you, Lord…
And I know I can't travel on this journey a single day without you,
there's too many external forces opposing me, a lot of internal ones too
You've reminded me numerous times that you're not going to leave me forsaken,
I'm holding on to that promise until I'm resting in your safe haven.

SENSE OF FAILURE

Sometimes I feel like I'm failing God when I decide to take actions desired by my flesh
instead of reviewing scriptures and consulting with fellow Christians to get through these tests
I feel like I'm failing my wife when I allow another woman's beauty to capture my attention
or when I allow impure thoughts to distract me from carrying-out God's mission
I feel like I'm failing my family and close-friends when I go months between contacting them
preventing me from offering my full support when they're feeling discouraged and condemned

I feel like I'm failing in my career and my walk with God because I'm not where I want to be,
But God... He always reminds me that I'm exactly where he wants me to be
He reminds me that despite the mistakes I make daily, I'm still covered by his love and mercy
He reminds me that He is the only one who could judge me and that he's already forgiven me
not only that, but He also washes away my sins and declares that I'm NOT GUILTY!!
and his son Jesus set me free from bondage, shame, guilt and sin when He died on that tree
Then He renews my courage and strength and commands me to continue his work
and be the strong ambassador that He's called on me to be.

Then I realized how some of my *failures* are seen as
successes in God's eyes...
I failed at being a "normal" person,
I failed at fitting-in with the crowd,
I failed at "staying inside the box",
I failed to remain "thinking inside the box",
I failed at being politically correct,
I failed at placing limitations on my life,
I failed at being all the things our society wants us to be...
But God made us all different,
So don't let the world tell you that you're a failure
because He's already given us the victory!!

Thank You, Lord

I would sometimes feel a bit overloaded
with all of the tasks that I have at hand,
trying to configure a healthy balance of being a great
Man of God, husband, business person, and friend
I've been discovering some disturbing knowledge
yet you've kept me in a peaceful state of mind,
I've encountered daily attacks from the enemy
yet you've enabled my heart to remain kind,
I've failed many of my life's tests
yet you've continually extended your grace,
I've mistreated many people, but I thank you for
holding back the deserving consequences of my mistakes
In fact, I'm taking a moment to thank you
for everything you've done for me, Lord,
I know I don't deserve your love and your blessings
but I thank you for allowing me to live for you, Lord.

CONVERSATION WITH LUCIFER

I stand toe-to-toe with you and I can't help but to laugh
in your face...
I see you and your army of demons lurking around my
peaceful place,
wishing I would slip-up and create an opportunity
for you to invade my personal space...
I see you glaring with hatred in your eyes as you have my
home encircled
shouting threats at me to the point where your face
turns purple,
Trying tirelessly to infiltrate my life-
throwing various temptations and insults my way
through people
to contaminate the roots of my soil so that it
becomes unfertile,
yet there's no way you can be in my circle.

You see, my circle has been created and protected
by God himself.
I got angels in my circle.
I got prayer warriors in my circle.
I got responsible Men of God in my circle.
I got respectable Virtuous Women in my circle.
I got former drug addicts in my circle.
I got former exotic dancers in my circle.
I got former pimps and prostitutes in my circle.
I got former inmates in my circle.
I got misfits and outsiders in my circle.
I got cancer survivors in my circle.
I got former gang members in my circle.

I got former alcoholics in my circle.
I got former victims of depression,
I got former victims of abuse,
former victims who've been stripped of their confidence
and have been physically and psychologically misused.
I see you tried to infiltrate my wife's life as well
but soon realized that attempt was of no good use,
because she's a praying Virtuous Woman herself
and all of her friends are Virtuous Women too!!

All the people in my circle didn't allow their valleys
to kill them
they stand stronger than ever today, ready to face any other forthcoming villain
So even if you did find a way into my circle, you wouldn't last too long
because you're not Built-God-Tough like we are!!
We face our problems head-on
yet you like to run and hide from your issues,
We let each other know when there's a clear problem
(face to face)
but you like to be sneaky and start rumors
You must've really pissed God-off
for Him to cast you out of heaven at lightning speed,
a place where you had everything you would ever need,
a place abundant in love, freedom, grace and mercy

A small part of me feels sorry for you—
because you're the only breathing vessel walking this earth
who has been eternally condemned,
Yet instead of admitting your faults and asking for
forgiveness

you take your anger out on us humans,
God's most valued creations,
and try to lead us astray so that we'll also be condemned—
Proof that misery truly does love company.
It's ok though, because some of us have already woke-up
and noticed your scheme,
God has already revealed to some of us your plans to
destroy everything,
God has already revealed to us what your future holds,
God has revealed that He has a purpose for each of us—
no matter how many demeaning things we've been told,
He has revealed that we are NOT failures,
that we do have a meaningful purpose in life,
that we still have a chance for forgiveness
no matter how many mistakes we've made in life,
that He loves us unconditionally
and doesn't hold grudges against us,
and He desires a personal relationship
with each and every one of us…

But you knew this already Satan,
and your plans would be dissolved
if the world were to be exposed to this truth.

THROWING STONES

I used to be one of the accusers,
one of the users and abusers,
I used to be a judgmental person
quick to throw in my opinion,
quick to throw stones at others
as if my sins were cleaner than others,
I used to point fingers and mock the unfortunate—
quick to label people as incompetent,
tried my hardest to fit-in with the crowds
still, my presence was hardly accepted and allowed…
I later realized that most of everyone else
saw something in me that I didn't even see in myself,
I was an outsider trying to "fit-in" all along
and it was when I accepted this that I felt the most calm,
I was soon loving on the same people I was once
throwing stones at
I even began defending them from others' vicious attacks,
I'm now one of the people who are sometimes frowned-upon
but I've experienced true freedom since I've accepted
God's Son.

LINES OF LIBERATION

The worries, the pain, the distractions, the fears
somehow all of it tends to become a vapor and disappears
when I open my notebook and write down all of the thoughts
that are constantly occurring in between my ears…

I get a taste of true freedom and liberation
when I express myself with just my pen and piece of paper
nobody has to get hurt or feel the wrath of my frustration
it's just me and God having numerous heart-to-heart
conversations…

I thank God for providing me this temporary escape from
all the madness,
the hurt, the guilt, the confusion, the pressure, and
all the sadness,
I know He gifted me with writing, yet it used to feel like a
curse to have this,
back when I tried to ignore my gift and was caught-up in my
"social status"

No matter what I'm battling or currently struggling with,
I can find liberation and peace by talking to God
and using my gift,
Now I'm looking for other writers & artists across the
country and within arm's length
with whom I can support and encourage to continue using
their God-given gifts.

Rebuilding Mode
(Outro)

The battle is finally over…
You've come-out on the other side victoriously…
You've obtained quite a few cuts and bruises
but those barriers no-longer stand before you…
You've obtained some burns from those fiery trials
but that fire didn't consume nor kill you…
You've expended all of the energy you had
into defeating your opposition
so now you're fatigued and probably wondering,
"What on earth do I do next?"
My suggestion: Ask God that very question.
He'll give you his instructions
and will restore your strength to carry them out…
He'll restore your joy and give you
a new level of comfort and peace…
He'll heal your wounds and will
allow your scars to encourage those who
look-up to you to follow in your footsteps…
He'll love on you…
He'll teach you how to forgive your opposition
and help you with the healing and recovery process…
He'll continually build your character—
but realize that all of this will take time.
Give God your time and trust his process.
You will not regret it.

ABOUT THE AUTHOR

    Roderick D. Talley is a creative writer and spoken word poet who values sharing the knowledge of God's love through his gifts and living by example. He looks to continue encouraging people of all backgrounds, learn from our past mistakes, and stay connected with our youth. Mr. Talley also owns and operates his book publishing company R.D. Talley Books Publishing, LLC and uses this company to build his brand of books and share business knowledge to fellow writers.

    He has one other professionally published poetry book entitled, "Sinner, Turned Role Model, Turned Advocate." He also has the first book of his underground poetry book series, "A Taste of the Creative Juices, Vol. 1" available. You're welcome to purchase his products and stay updated with Mr. Talley's events, giveaways, upcoming book releases, book reviews, poetry videos and promotional merchandise through his website and social media pages listed below.

Website: www.rdtalleybooks.com

Instagram: roderickthewriter

Facebook: Author Roderick D. Talley

YouTube: R.D. Talley Books Publishing

www.ingramcontent.com/pod-product-compliance
Lightning Source LLC
Chambersburg PA
CBHW021124080526
44587CB00010B/630